AS THE CROW FLIES

Poems: 1996–2017

George Monteiro

BRICKTOP
2017

Copyright © 2017 by George Monteiro

All rights reserved under International and Pan-American Copyright Conventions.

Bricktop Hill Books
PO Box 1016
Willimantic, CT 06226

Library of Congress Control Number: 2017940172

ISBN 10: 0997366931

ISBN 13: 9780997366938

There were three ra'ens sat on a tree,
Down a down, hay down, hay down,
There were as black as black might be;
With a down. Then one of them said to his mate,
Where shall we our breakfast take?
With a down, derry, derry, derry down, down

"The Three Ravens" (Child Ballad)

Dec. 25/ 96

Black birds walk fallow fields.

May 23/ 97

**When the hawk runs high
the crow lives close to me.**

June 22/ 97

These birds
pace and strut.
They sit in trees.
Cawing and crowing,
bothering one another
in frenetic chase,
they wingspread
across the lights
I look out of.
Just as suddenly
as they have entered,
they end the show
in this place—
for now, since
they are always
a holdover,
a running act.
The crows of Windham
do not wear the colors
of the spirit.

June 23/ 97

These, too, are birds
of Connecticut.
Not here this morning,
though, are the crows.
Emily's wind chimes
hang loose off the deck.
One smaller bird flies,
almost silently, through
the trees. I see its near-
silence. The flowers stand
as if waiting. The leaves
of trees respond to persuasion,
all things rocking still.
Nothing seems to signify;
the crow flies or walks
its own shadow, to be
sure, but today
does it elsewhere.
When they are not here
I know they are derivative
of the real and elsewhere
manageable, though best
so in absentia.
My birds are
east-of-the-river
stiffs, itinerant,
but not nomadic,
wage-earners
drawing pay at

end of day to
frustrate any
thoughts of
garnish.

June 24/ 97

The crows of Windham
—not here again.
The air is close and
they are nowhere to
be seen, nowhere heard.
Their absence is no
presence, not even
when I think about
them or succeed in
recalling their crowing,
their unregulated cavorting,
the pure lines of their self-
absorption, putting on
a show that needs
work but won't get it.
Solitary birds hit the trees
and the calico stray
leaves the deck.
Stillness, humidity,
heavy air, promise
no crow. The temperature
and weather have nothing
to do with their caprice.
I can learn about crows
if I watch these crows, if
I take what nature gives me.

June 25/ 97

It is the gray, pencil-lead morning I had fancied in the minutes before I got up to shower. There's more light but the stillness is palpable and there are no birds to be seen, no sounds to be heard save the cicadas (a guess) and a fading car siren. Where are my crows? Whose yard do they animate this morning? Mowing the grass and weeds, as I did yesterday, invariably brings birds who feast on the new exposure, but today they stay away, maybe because it's Wednesday, the professionals' day off. Whose crows are they today? The sirens stop, stop. Nobody predicts anything.

June 26/ 97

Crows do not crow to themselves.
Crows crow indirectly at one
another, each squawk an order,
complaint, a rough intimacy.
They are not a parliament of
fowls, nor a college of clerics.
Rather more like a Service
Master cleaning team with
the house all to themselves,
knowing that, work done,
they'll move on, knowing
that the work itself is an end,
no matter where or when
it takes place. But the crows
do no work. They boss, they
inspect, they cover ground,
they look alert, act busy, size
things up, take soundings of
unexpected shallows, launch
commuter flights of no duration,
and feed most offhandedly, working it all out beforehand, of course.

June 27/ 97

Yesterday I saw crows
walking a yard on Bricktop
Road, only two or three of them,
an avant-garde or a rear-guard,
it was not clear. Harbinger
or vestige? Remnant or
sample? They haven't been
here for nearly a week,
to my knowledge.
Hark, a croak, repeated,
even as I write, drives
a squirrel along a branch,
deep into a tree. And
now I see them, flying
out of the tree, first
one, then a second,
and I know there are more.
They do not walk the ground.
They're gone, just like that,
a courtesy call, passing
through, confirming air rights.

June 28/ 97

**No crows today.
Let them come
when they will.
They satisfy
no need here.**

July 15/ 97

There are late afternoon birds
that won't be here in the fall.
They are small, they are quick,
they stay low to the ground,
disdaining the high branch
flights that criss-and-cross
when there's a schedule to keep.
These late afternoon birds
put on shows for themselves.
What was amusing amuses no
more. What was funny
strikes another note now.
Like Nature, History wears
the color of the spirit and the
spirit has no will.

Feb. 9/ 98

**The crows outside
my window show leg
on the wing, teasing,
but only once a day.**

Feb. 15/ 98

**Towards noon
the high-flying birds
move their shadows
across the winter
grass.**

May 4/ 98

Take no shit from a bird.

Aug. 26/ 98

With two-thirds of the summer gone, in late August return the crows, following a night of tropical thunder and heavy rain, to signal a change in season and prospects to count on.

Nov. 9/ 98

**The crows of Windham,
a subset, real but actual,
come in the mildness of
this given autumn, as
one, in twos or threes.
They bask, relax, mind
their p's and q's, vet
the grounds for future
landings. Sundown
sees them go. Sun-
down, they are gone.**

Nov. 23/ 98

They do not come today either,
having pretty much stayed away
for weeks—two at least—as they
check out the world elsewhere.
I'm annoyed because I have the
urge to write about them—here—
not in their conspicuous absence.

Mar. 17/ 99

The crows fly overhead
where they menace less.
I do not look up at them.
Then I do and I see one.
They craw and croak,
glad that spring is just
about here with only a
reminder of Monday's
snowstorm left over
to keep them honest
as to who's boss.

June 8/ 99

Mid-dawn they come
to foot the empty streets,
their colors muted to a
dull dark, their sounds silent.
They do not feed, do not water.
Alert commandos at patrol,
Tupamaros taking this Vila
Carlos Paz for an afternoon
to show that they can.
They disappear through
the big hole in the sky.
No one sees their going,
these gossips in flight.

June 9/ 99

Even the punctual arrival
of the first crow is a sham.
It swoops in and it sweeps out,
showing only the will to
have done with it. Others
will come, land, and walk
the street, cross-hatch
the beat, and then carry
themselves aloft to still
barely greening pastures.
What they do they did
when milk stood in bottles
before doors shut against
the night, and sacks of bread,
too. Still, even the seeming
perdurable black birds give
no simple or easy guarantee.

June 28/ 99

A low-flying black bird,
what prey do you seek
at that altitude? Or
do you wish only to
bring early morning
sobriety to the not
yet startled grass or
its fractious minions?
Even birds have their
early risers, self-starters
worth their salt at
getting a jump on a day,
playing nice to the world
or giving fair warning
to the discovered worm
that they are about to pass.

Aug. 24/ 99

My crows walk tough this midmorning, thinking drought and hurricane thoughts. It's time to assess, report, record for the sake of history, another year's still turning, the beat familiar and, considering, in good shape. The jays are coming; they always come.

Aug. 30/ 99

Cawing at a distance,
the sound coming
through shades drawn
against the daylight gray
I know is out there,
along with the leaves
of autumn, the first
to be grounded.

Sept. 2/ 99

Crow sounds this morning
just after six, well after
the still-in-the-dark delivery
of the *Hartford Courant*,
a newspaper that promotes
itself as the country's
longest continuous running
daily. As for the crow, no
matter; it's like contemplating
apples and oranges. The crow
sounds stop and a barely
broken quiet settles in until
the alarm rings in for real.
The latest reawakening and, today,
to the recovery of what humans call
trash. No one steals their good
name, if good it is. No white trash
here.

Sept. 2/ 99

Crows talk trash among
themselves when their wings
serve them mainly for cover
and walking ballast. A peri-
patetic committee, an itinerant
comitatus, each one an American
judge, in these parts, following
his circuit of tryouts, his court
of appeals. Repetition, not love,
calls us to the tunes of this world.

Sept. 2/ 99

If the crow is a poet,
then the crow's style,
as Frost might say,
lies in the way it takes
itself. Crowing as it
does, it does not know
to crow. When all of
it is crow, there is no
crow to speak of.

Sept. 5/ 99

The size of it and the sound made by this startled bird startled me, seeing black swiftly, up close.

Oct. 3/ 99

Of late they tell us these
black birds bring death
and my saying, if I believe
them, grows old, grows
cold. Even more darkly
significant are they, though
try as I do, I can hear no
change in the squawk,
see no difference in their
stride. They obviously
hold to the long view of
things, a bird's eye view
of the here and now.

Oct. 5/ 99

May the poet of the jar stand us
in good stead when the eleven
o'clock news pictures for us black
birds laid out in a row on a table,
awaiting autopsy, confirmation of
death by air-borne disease con-
tagious to human beings in this and
other parts of Connecticut. An early
frost will kill off the awful threat,
along with other living things, the
meteorologist promises, for the
season.

Dec. 3/ 99

On my left they scatter up
into flight when I go out for
the morning paper. They
give off no sign of scare,
emblematic of nothing at all.

Dec. 4/ 99

Dropping down to feed,
carpeting the front yard
then thudding off to
wing it God knows where,
a squadron of dark maenads
dapple the sunlight.
Later on, crows gone,
familiar black birds,
two or three of them,
drop down squat to step
off this picked-over
place as if they alone
know some single thing
that is flat-out true.

Dec. 16/ 99

**today
pas de deux
con brio**

Jan. 21-22/ 00

They big-
body down
to Bricktop,
a highway
that spawns
no road kill
to speak of.

Feb. 26/ 00

**In spit-shine strut
or soundless fly-by,
dazzling in sunlight or
in preen-drizzle sheen,
the black bird prospers.**

Autumn/ 00

Raking leaves
away from the
stone wall and
out into the street
for trash pickup
on an appointed
day, I also rake
out a pair of black
wings, though not
enough else of a
body to move me
to signal those alert
to the potential in
this matter. I take
the chance. I tell
no one.

Dec. 7/ 00

**A day of snow keeps
them all elsewhere.**

June 27/ 01

**Crows double
up on dry leaf-
less branches,
bouncing hard
on these still
attached sticks
until one of them
snaps with one
bird hanging
fast till it breaks
free and then
up it swoops,
handling still
its freight—
the bough breaks
as the crow flies
& it will not fall.**

July 7/ 01

**wings entire,
in full spread,
friction-flat**

July 20/ 01

**seldom congregating early
coming when they like
throwing their parties
taking their constitutionals
fussing less than the pigeon**

Sept. 10/ 01

Darkening the darkness, it moves the shadow along, or, rather, it darkens the moving shadow in which it walks.

Nov. 20/ 01

**Black birds hop
over the leaves
piling up in the
gutter.**

Apr. 22/ 02

**Halfway up in the still leafless tree
—all of it dead at last—crows in
tandem cast fluttering shadows,
scorning, as ever, the not-yet-empty
larder of the backyard feeder.**

May 1/ 02

In the backyard a crow
will make do with a tree.
It sits still and does not
watch until, dropping off,
it settles on its shadow,
and commences to pick-
peck and swallow whole.

Nov. 8/ 02

A left-over crow
walking the road,
up and down,
to and fro, think-
ing, thinking—
thinking what?

Jan. 22/03

In this winter of no winter
they Blackhawk down to
peck away at the threadbare
earth for worms and bugs
and other bone-building
beings. Pickings are slim
but they betray no impatience
or signal disappointment,
for the Lord will provide
as long as they keep doing
what they do. And now,
as sudden as the drop,
they're up, up and away.

Apr. 1/ 07

Black draws down to black,
pointing me to a driveway
in need of re-surfacing.

Aug. 7/ 07

**They are one to ten this year,
maybe as few as one to the score.
So many gone, so many.**

Aug. 18/ 07

The Windham crow faces nothing.

Feb. 26/ 09

Those that come now are bigger,
heavier and, presumably, stronger,
proof, perhaps, that the survival of
the fittest holds true, but no longer
flying in flocks, though as I write I
spy 'twa corbies, each to each,
fidgeting over something I cannot
see.

Mar. 23/ 09

**crowing
evermore
evermore
never more
than now**

June 29/ 10

There's been a sea change in their behavior. Three times now, I have startled them into flight as I have opened the door to go out to fetch the paper. Growing back slowly in number, down from their peak, generously a dozen to twenty, but up to a promising count of six to eight, they look for bugs in the weeds thick and thin, no longer displaying themselves on the pavements—driveway and road—or yackity-yacking in the foliage of a tall and steadfast oak.

July 6/ 10

I'm called to the window to see the crows walking with familiarity the street of their racial memory, one supposes, once more taking dominion, one step at a time, for the duration of a birdbrain's attention.

Apr. 4/ 12

There are more of them about now. Nature's largess. This species lives for the nonce.

Oct. 2/ 14

The crow quits.

Nov. 21/ 14

**Over and again a crow
rides a lid down the side
of a snow-slicked roof.
Crows will be crows.**

Jan. 6 / 15

**Would it see
a sign, this one
crow turning
over ground-
leaves left over
from the fall?**

Nov. 29 / 15

**Rare now as hen's teeth.
Well, not quite.**

Nov. 17 / 15

A crow solos into the middle of
the street, barely glances at the
leaf piles scattered here and there,
and walks out of view. No more
touch-down, cast no discernible
shadow and without a howdy-do
fly off. Good. Shoo. Go away.

Nov. 21 / 15

They do not land, but from their shadow moving deftly along the ground I see them.

Dec. 1 / 15

They're back in numbers today, well 6 and 1 or 2 more. A squirrel frets them but they will not scare. They stay for a bit and then fly.

Dec. 7 / 15

**Here, in numbers, at 8:25 a.m.
Where were you all summer?**

Dec. 9 / 15

Now the crows
and the bluejays
are one to ten.
Like Frost, I
estimate.

Dec. 13 / 15

an unheard choir
waddles before
a red front door
spreading wings
into emptiness
when a car turns
into the drive

Dec. 15 / 15

The wide-winged hawk vies
with the crow for dominion
over this winter-growth lawn.

Dec. 21 / 15

Swiftly flies the crow past my
window, landing softly in the tree.
Soon others drop down to the street.

Dec. 29 / 15

The single-o crow comes and touches down, but there's no need to dwell on an impulse.

Dec. 31 / 15

Crows in the backyard, foraging in the leaves, corner a lone squirrel, who suddenly attacks, sending them fluttering and flapping upwards about six inches off the ground, and then runs to the end of the yard.

Jan. 1 / 16

The crow, I think, does not fly in formation. It will, however, deign to join a congeries at ground level.

Jan. 15 / 16

Sun and clouds today and the crows cavort. Later, a single one sucks water from a small patch of ice before the recycle bin.

Jan. 25 / 16

Outside my window the year's first robins rest nervously on branches before taking wing for parts north. Other birds fly in, cast shadows, followed by a solitary cardinal. The crow takes its bloody time. Meanwhile, more robins. The robins persist.

Jan. 26 / 16

**At noon it's quiet in the tree.
No red, no blue, no black.
At 2 they return, one by one.**

Jan. 29 / 16

It pokes its beak at a hole in the snow. Another one does the same, and then another, *unsoweiter*. They do not appear to be thirsty or hungry. Killing time.

Feb. 6 / 16

A moving shadow on the bright snow is not so black as the swoops of bird.

Feb. 10 / 16

Under a gray sky a modest murder of crows cavorting in a snow-covered street beyond the window lingers away.

Feb. 19 / 16

Crows, more crows, frenzy flights, in and out of view. Gone.

Feb. 20 / 16

**Not a crow today.
They gambol some-
where else.**

Apr. 5 / 16

**No birds this morning,
not even crows, after
a day of falling snow.**

Dec. 15 / 16

too cold for the crow

Dec. 25 / 16

Call them 'colly birds' I learn today, a name deriving from an old word for 'coal,' but still they do not come, ready or not.

Jan. 29 / 17

I watch crows picking away at winter scrub down in the backyard and think of how best to render the scene.

Mar. 27 / 17

Crows walk, step by step, to the woods, risking the shortest route possible, even tramping straight through the middle of a for-the-moment puddle in the middle of this rain-soaked front yard.

Mar. 28 / 17

Two crows walk into water pooled above a plugged-up street drain. Gather ye rosebuds while you may.

Apr. 3 / 17

My three corbies like the street out front. One time out of a 100 they land in the backyard. It's lower and they don't like lower. They stand now in a perfect row in the street facing the yard, toeing the line, with a precision seen only in an attentive military. The spaces between them are exact, compass-drawn. They are not making a visit. Surely they prefer to stand (or walk). After all, there's nowhere they need go, they all but say. But, alas, they must, on the silent crack of the moment, fly away, each to trace its own flight pattern, staying the course of a course not approved or sanctioned, but natural as a croak.

Apr. 10 / 17

—Sir?
What's
fit for
the bird
that will
come on
a silver
platter
under a
silver
cover?
No? No
choice?
None?
Water,
maybe?
Vichy?
Evian?
Drops
from a
dipper?
Nothing
goes with
Crow?
Try Poe,
you say?
Old Crow?
Hemlock?
He'll try

it himself?
When he
shakes
election-
day dirt
forever?

About the Author

George Monteiro is the author of three previous volumes of poetry, *The Coffee Exchange*, *Double Weaver's Knot*, and *The Pessoa Chronicles*. He has also published translations of the poetry of Jorge de Sena, Miguel Torga, Pedro da Silveira, and Fernando Pessoa, and the prose of José Rodrigues Miguéis and José Saramago. He and his wife make their home in Connecticut.

www.ingramcontent.com/pod-product-compliance
Lightning Source LLC
Chambersburg PA
CBHW031455040426
42444CB00007B/1107